Test Talk
Practice Book

Editorial Offices: Glenview, Illinois • Parsippany, New Jersey • New York, New York
Sales Offices: Parsippany, New Jersey • Duluth, Georgia • Glenview, Illinois •
Coppell, Texas • Ontario, California • Mesa, Arizona

www.sfsocialstudies.com

ISBN 0-328-04111-4

8 9 10-V004-11 10 09 08 07 06 05

© Scott Foresman 5

Contents

Overview

Overview Passage 1
Locate Key Words in the Question 2
Locate Key Words in the Text 3
Choose the Right Answer 4
Use Information from the Text 5
Use Information from Graphics 6
Write Your Answer to Score High 7

Unit 1

Unit 1 Passage 8
Locate Key Words in the Question 9
Locate Key Words in the Text 10
Choose the Right Answer 11
Use Information from the Text 12
Use Information from Graphics 13
Write Your Answer to Score High 14

Unit 2

Unit 2 Passage 15
Locate Key Words in the Question 16
Locate Key Words in the Text 17
Choose the Right Answer 18
Use Information from the Text 19
Use Information from Graphics 20
Write Your Answer to Score High 21

Unit 3

Unit 3 Passage 22
Locate Key Words in the Question 23
Locate Key Words in the Text 24
Choose the Right Answer 25
Use Information from the Text 26
Use Information from Graphics 27
Write Your Answer to Score High 28

Unit 4

Unit 4 Passage 29
Locate Key Words in the Question 30
Locate Key Words in the Text 31
Choose the Right Answer 32
Use Information from the Tex 33
Use Information from Graphics 34
Write Your Answer to Score High 35

Unit 5

Unit 5 Passage 36
Locate Key Words in the Question 37
Locate Key Words in the Text 38
Choose the Right Answer 39
Use Information from the Text 40
Use Information from Graphics 41
Write Your Answer to Score High 42

Unit 6

Unit 6 Passage 43
Locate Key Words in the Question........... 44
Locate Key Words in the Text.................. 45
Choose the Right Answer 46
Use Information from the Text 47
Use Information from Graphics 48
Write Your Answer to Score High 49

Unit 8

Unit 8 Passage 57
Locate Key Words in the Question........... 58
Locate Key Words in the Text.................. 59
Choose the Right Answer 60
Use Information from the Text 61
Use Information from Graphics 62
Write Your Answer to Score High 63

Unit 7

Unit 7 Passage 50
Locate Key Words in the Question........... 51
Locate Key Words in the Text.................. 52
Choose the Right Answer 53
Use Information from the Text 54
Use Information from Graphics 55
Write Your Answer to Score High 56

Unit 9

Unit 9 Passage 64
Locate Key Words in the Question........... 65
Locate Key Words in the Text.................. 66
Choose the Right Answer 67
Use Information from the Text 68
Use Information from Graphics 69
Write Your Answer to Score High 70

Name _____ Date _____

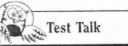
American People, American Land

Directions: Read about this citizen hero. Then follow the directions on pages 2–7.

Protecting the Land

1   Like most children growing up in Custer County, Oklahoma, Mike Harris loved being outdoors. By the time he was nine, Mike had roamed every inch of his family's ranch.

2   With his deep love of the land came a fierce urge to protect it. When Mike saw trash floating in a rain-filled ditch, he got angry. He knew he had to do something. While only in third grade, Mike started a group called Environmental CPR. The letters stood for Conserve, Preserve, Reserve. The group's goal was to clean up the countryside and teach other young people about pollution and its dangers.

3   But Mike faced a challenge. Because he was shy, he found it hard to speak out. However, with his mom's strong support, Mike was able to overcome his fears. He says: "I took responsibility and did what needed to be done. When your heart's into it, nothing will stop you."

4   Mike worked hard to promote his cause. He spoke out at county speech contests. He passed out fliers, led recycling drives, and even appeared on radio and TV.

5   His efforts paid off. In its first few years, Environmental CPR collected and recycled more than 22,000 pounds of trash—about the weight of five sport utility vehicles.

6   Of course, Mike could not do all this himself. Environmental CPR was a success because Mike Harris inspired the same sense of responsibility in several thousand people. In fact, the project continued for ten years under his leadership and spread out across the entire state. Today it continues its work on behalf of the environment.

Test Talk

Use with Overview.

Strategy 1 Locate Key Words in the Question

Directions: Before you can answer a question, you need to understand the question. Follow these steps to understand the question.

- Read the question.

- Ask yourself: "**Who** or **what** is the question about?" Words that tell "who" or "what" are **key words**. Circle key words.

- Look for and circle other key words. Often question words and other important words are key words.

- Turn the question into a statement using key words. Follow this model: "I need to find out _____."

Learn

Read the question. Circle the key words and complete the sentence.

1. (What) do the letters in Environmental (CPR) (stand) (for)?

    ⊙ A Cardio, Preserve, Reserve

    ⊙ B Conservation, Preservation, Reservation

    ⊙ C Conserve, Preserve, Reserve

    ⊙ D Conserve, Prevent, Repair

    Circle key words.

    I need to find out what the letters in Environmental CPR stand for.

    Turn the question into a statement using key words.

Try It

Read each question. Circle the key words and complete each sentence.

2. How did Mike promote his cause?

    ⊙ A He bought a radio and TV.

    ⊙ B He appeared on radio and TV.

    ⊙ C He sold his radio and TV.

    ⊙ D He stopped watching radio and TV.

    I need to find out _____

    _____

3. Why was Environmental CPR a success? Use details from the text to support your answer.

    I need to find out _____

    _____

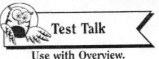

Strategy 2 Locate Key Words in the Text

Directions: You can also understand a question by thinking about where you need to look for the answer. Follow these steps to understand the question.

- Read the question.
- Look for and circle key words in the question.
- Look for and circle key words in the text that match key words in the question.
- Decide where to look for the answer.
  - ➤ To find the answer, you may have to **look in one place in the text**. The answer is *right there* in the text.
  - ➤ To find the answer, you may have to **look in several places in the text**. You have to *think and search* for information.
  - ➤ To find the answer, you may have to **combine what you know with what the author tells you**. The answer comes from *the author and you*.

Learn

Read the question. Circle the key words and complete the sentence.

1. Based on paragraphs 5 and 6, (how) did (Mike's) (efforts) (pay) (off)? Use details from the text to support your answer.

   I found the answer in _paragraph 5, sentence 2, and_

   paragraph 6, sentences 2–4.

- Look for and circle key words in the question.
- Look for and circle key words in the text that match key words in the question.

- The question asks you to tell how Mike's efforts paid off.
- You will have to **look in several places in the text** for information.

Try It

Read each question. Circle the key words and complete each sentence.

2. Based on paragraph 4, how did Mike promote his cause?
   - ⬭ **A** He bought a radio and TV.
   - ⬭ **B** He appeared on radio and TV.
   - ⬭ **C** He sold his radio and TV.
   - ⬭ **D** He stopped watching radio and TV.

   I found the answer in _____

   _____

3. Why could nothing stop Mike's efforts? Use details from the text to support your answer.

   I found the answer in _____

   _____

Strategy 3 Choose the Right Answer

Directions: Use this strategy for a multiple-choice question in which you need to choose the best answer. Follow these steps to answer a multiple-choice question.

- Read the question.
- Read each answer choice.
- Rule out any choice you know is wrong. Go back to the text to rule out other choices.
- Mark your answer choice.
- Check your answer by comparing it with the text.

Learn

Cross out any choice you know is wrong. Next, go back to the text to rule out any other choices. Then mark your answer choice.

1. Who started Environmental CPR?

    ⬭ A   ~~young people~~

    ⬭ B   ~~Mike's mom~~

    ⬬ C   Mike Harris

    ⬭ D   ~~thousands of people~~

    > You will have to **look in one place in the text**.

    > Rule out the incorrect choices. Choose answer C because the text supports this choice.

Try It

Cross out any choice you know is wrong. Next, go back to the text to rule out any other choices. Then mark your answer choice.

2. What do the letters in Environmental CPR stand for?

    ⬭ A   Cardio, Preserve, Reserve

    ⬭ B   Conservation, Preservation, Reservation

    ⬭ C   Conserve, Preserve, Reserve

    ⬭ D   Conserve, Prevent, Repair

3. How did Mike promote his cause?

    ⬭ A   He bought a radio and TV.

    ⬭ B   He appeared on radio and TV.

    ⬭ C   He sold his radio and TV.

    ⬭ D   He stopped watching radio and TV.

Strategy 4 Use Information from the Text

Directions: A question may tell you to support your answer with details from the text. If it does, then you must include information from the text. Follow these steps to answer such questions.

- Read the question.
- Look for and circle key words in the question.
- **Make notes** about details from the text that answer the question.
- Reread the question and your notes.
- If details are missing, go back to the text.

Learn

Use information from the text to answer the question.

1. (How) did (Mike) (promote) his (cause)? Use details from the text to support your answer.

   My Notes: ~~overcame his fears~~, promote cause,

   speech contests, fliers, recycling drives,

   radio, TV

   My Answer: Mike promoted his cause by speaking

   in contests, handing out fliers, leading recycling drives,

   and appearing on radio and TV.

- Look for and circle key words in the question.
- The question asks for the ways that Mike promoted his cause.
- Read the text and **make notes** about how Mike promoted his cause.

Reread the question and cross out any notes that do not apply to the question.

Answer the question in your own words.

Try It

Use information from the text to answer the question.

2. How did Mike's sense of responsibility help his cause? Use details from the text to support your answer.

   My Notes: _____

   _____

   _____

   My Answer: _____

   _____

   _____

   _____

Strategy 5 Use Information from Graphics

Directions: A question may ask you about a photograph or tell you to support your answer with details from a photograph. If it does, then you must include information about the photograph. Follow these steps to answer questions about the photograph.

- Read the question.
- Look for and circle key words in the question.
- Use what you know to analyze the photograph.
- Use details from the photograph to answer the question.

Learn

Look at the photograph on page 1. Use information from the photograph to answer the question.

1. Based on the photograph, (how) are the (children) (helping) the (environment)? Use details to support your answer.

    To find the answer, I will look at the photograph of

    the five children.

    | Look for and circle key words in the question. |

    My Answer: The children are picking up litter.

    | Look at page 1. Analyze the photograph. Use details to answer the question. |

Try It

Look at the photograph on page 1. Use information from the photograph to answer the question.

2. Based on the photograph, what environment are the children improving? Use details to support your answer.

    To find the answer, I will _____

    _____

    _____

    My Answer: _____

    _____

    _____

    _____

© Scott Foresman 5

Strategy 6 Write Your Answer to Score High

Directions: A question may tell you to write an answer. Follow these steps to write a correct, complete, and focused answer.

- Read the question.
- Make notes about details that answer the question.
- Reread the question and your notes. If details are missing, go back to the text.
- Begin your answer with words from the question. Include details from your notes.
- Check your answer. Ask yourself:
  - ➤ Is my answer correct? Are some details incorrect?
  - ➤ Is my answer complete? Do I need to add more details?
  - ➤ Is my answer focused? Do all my details help answer the question?

Learn

Examine this sample done by an imaginary student named Darlene. Analyze Darlene's work. Cross out incorrect or unfocused information. What should she do to score higher?

1. (How) did (Mike) (promote) his (cause)? Use details from the text to support your answer.

   | Darlene circled key words in the question. |

   Darlene's Notes: ~~overcame his fears~~, speech contests, fliers, recycling drives, radio, TV, Web sites

   | Darlene's notes include unfocused information. |

   Darlene's Answer: Mike overcame his fears. Mike promoted his cause by speaking in contests, handing out fliers, leading recycling drives, and appearing on radio, TV, and Web sites.

   | Darlene's notes are incorrect. |

   To score higher, Darlene needs to _cross out information about overcoming fears, and delete "Web sites" because it is incorrect._

Try It

Examine this sample done by an imaginary student named José. Analyze José's work. Cross out incorrect or unfocused information. What should he do to score higher?

2. How did Mike's sense of responsibility help his cause? Use details from the text to support your answer.

   José's Notes: inspire responsibility, several million people, spread out, same goal

   José's Answer: Mike's sense of responsibility helped his cause by setting an example for millions of people. His group spread statewide. Today his goal is the same.

   To score higher, José needs to _____

   _____

Early Life, East and West

Directions: Read about this research skill. Then follow the directions on pages 9–14.

Internet Research

1
You can find out more about a subject by doing research. Research is a way of gathering information to help solve a problem. Many people use books in the library for research. They may also use the Internet. The Internet is a worldwide network of computers linked together. On the Internet, information can be viewed and shared in on-screen pages called Web sites. A Web site can be set up by a company, school, government, or individual.

2
You can use search engines to find information on the Internet. A search engine is a computer site that searches for information. Search engines will lead you to other Web sites.

3
You can do a search by typing in a word or phrase. Say you want information on the Cheyenne. You may know there is also a city named Cheyenne, but you want information on the Native American group. Type in "the Cheyenne" in quotation marks. The quotation marks tell that the topic you want is a complete phrase.

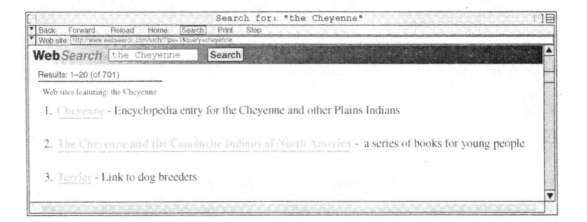

Strategy 1 Locate Key Words in the Question

Directions: Before you can answer a question, you need to understand the question. Follow these steps to understand the question.

- Read the question.

- Ask yourself: "**Who** or **what** is the question about?" Words that tell "who" or "what" are **key words**. Circle key words.

- Look for and circle other key words. Often question words and other important words are key words.

- Turn the question into a statement using key words. Follow this model: "I need to find out _____."

Learn

Read the question. Circle the key words and complete the sentence.

1. (What) is the (Internet)?

     ○ **A** on-screen pages

     ○ **B** a worldwide network of computers linked together

     ○ **C** a computer site that searches for information

     ○ **D** a fast computer

I need to find out _what the Internet is._

> Circle key words.

> Turn the question into a statement using key words.

Try It

Read each question. Circle the key words and complete each sentence.

2. Where will search engines lead you?

     ○ **A** to other Web sites

     ○ **B** to the library

     ○ **C** to the teacher

     ○ **D** to Cheyenne, Wyoming

I need to find out _____

_____

3. Why might you put a topic in quotation marks? Use details from the text to support your answer.

I need to find out _____

_____

Strategy 2 **Locate Key Words in the Text**

Directions: You can also understand a question by thinking about where you need to look for the answer. Follow these steps to understand the question.

- Read the question.
- Look for and circle key words in the question.
- Look for and circle key words in the text that match key words in the question.
- Decide where to look for the answer.
  - ➤ To find the answer, you may have to **look in one place in the text**. The answer is *right there* in the text.
  - ➤ To find the answer, you may have to **look in several places in the text**. You have to *think and search* for information.
  - ➤ To find the answer, you may have to **combine what you know with what the author tells you**. The answer comes from *the author and you*.

Learn

Read the question. Circle the key words and complete the sentence.

1. Based on paragraph 1, who can set up a Web site? Use details from the text to support your answer.

   I found the answer in paragraph 1, sentence 7.

- Look for and circle key words in the question.
- Look for and circle key words in the text that match key words in the question.

- The question asks you to identify who can set up a Web site.
- You will have to **look in one place in the text** for information.

Try It

Read each question. Circle the key words and complete each sentence.

2. Based on paragraph 2, where will search engines lead you?
   - ⬭ **A** to other Web sites
   - ⬭ **B** to the library
   - ⬭ **C** to the teacher
   - ⬭ **D** to Cheyenne, Wyoming

   I found the answer in ——————————————————————————

   ——

3. Why might you put a topic in quotation marks? Use details from the text to support your answer.

   I found the answer in ——————————————————————————

   ——

Strategy 3 Choose the Right Answer

Directions: Use this strategy for a multiple-choice question in which you need to choose the best answer. Follow these steps to answer a multiple-choice question.

> - Read the question.
> - Read each answer choice.
> - Rule out any choice you know is wrong. Go back to the text to rule out other choices.
> - Mark your answer choice.
> - Check your answer by comparing it with the text.

Learn

Cross out any choice you know is wrong. Next, go back to the text to rule out any other choices. Then mark your answer choice.

1. What is the Internet?
   - ○ A on-screen pages
   - ● B a worldwide network of computers linked together
   - ○ C a computer site that searches for information
   - ○ D a fast computer

> You will have to **look in one place in the text**.

> Rule out the incorrect choices. Choose answer B because the text supports this choice.

Try It

Cross out any choice you know is wrong. Next, go back to the text to rule out any other choices. Then mark your answer choice.

2. Who can set up a Web site?
   - ○ A only a company or school
   - ○ B a company, school, or government but not an individual
   - ○ C a company, school, government, or individual
   - ○ D an individual but not a company, school, or government

3. Where will search engines lead you?
   - ○ A to other Web sites
   - ○ B to the library
   - ○ C to the teacher
   - ○ D to Cheyenne, Wyoming

Strategy 4 Use Information from the Text

Directions: A question may tell you to support your answer with details from the text. If it does, then you must include information from the text. Follow these steps to answer such questions.

- Read the question.
- Look for and circle key words in the question.
- **Make notes** about details from the text that answer the question.
- Reread the question and your notes.
- If details are missing, go back to the text.

Learn

Use information from the text to answer the question.

1. (What) is the (Internet)? Use details from the text to support your answer.

   My Notes: ~~research information~~, Internet,

   worldwide network of computers, linked together

   My Answer: The Internet is a network of computers

   around the world that are linked together.

- Look for and circle key words in the question.
- The question asks for a definition of Internet.
- Read the text and **make notes** about what the Internet is.

Reread the question and cross out any notes that do not apply to the question.

Answer the question in your own words.

Try It

Use information from the text to answer the question.

2. What can you do to find information on the Cheyenne but not the city named Cheyenne? Use details from the text to support your answer.

   My Notes: _____

   _____

   _____

   My Answer: _____

   _____

   _____

   _____

© Scott Foresman 5

Strategy 5 Use Information from Graphics

Directions: A question may ask you about a picture or tell you to support your answer with details from a picture. If it does, then you must include information about the picture. Follow these steps to answer questions about the picture.

- Read the question.
- Look for and circle key words in the question.
- Use what you know to analyze the picture.
- Use details from the picture to answer the question.

Learn

Look at the picture of a computer screen on page 8. Use information from the picture to answer the question.

1. Based on the sample computer screen, (what) are the (Web sites) featuring the word ("Cheyenne")? Use details to support your answer.

   > Look for and circle key words in the question.

   To find the answer, I will *go back to the computer*

   screen and look for the list of Web sites.

   My Answer: *The Web sites are "Cheyenne," "The Cheyenne and the Comanche Indians of North America," and "Terrier."*

   > Look at page 8. Analyze the computer screen. Use details to answer the question.

Try It

Look at the picture of a computer screen on page 8. Use information from the picture to answer the question.

2. Based on the sample computer screen, how is the first Web site described? Use details to support your answer.

   To find the answer, I will _____

   _____

   _____

   My Answer: _____

   _____

   _____

   _____

Strategy 6 Write Your Answer to Score High

Directions: A question may tell you to write an answer. Follow these steps to write a correct, complete, and focused answer.

- Read the question.
- Make notes about details that answer the question.
- Reread the question and your notes. If details are missing, go back to the text.
- Begin your answer with words from the question. Include details from your notes.
- Check your answer. Ask yourself:
  - ➤ Is my answer correct? Are some details incorrect?
  - ➤ Is my answer complete? Do I need to add more details?
  - ➤ Is my answer focused? Do all my details help answer the question?

Learn

Examine this sample done by an imaginary student named Doria. Analyze Doria's work. Cross out unfocused information. What should she do to score higher?

1. Why is the Internet useful for doing research? Use details from the text to support your answer.

   | Doria circled key words in the question. |

   Doria's Notes: ~~books in library useful too~~, information on Web sites, set up by company, person

   | Doria's notes include unfocused information. |

   Doria's Answer: The Internet is useful for research. Books in libraries are useful too. On the Internet, you can find information from a company or person.

   | Doria's information is incomplete. |

   To score higher, Doria needs to cross out unfocused information about books, and add

   that a government or school can also set up a site to make the answer complete.

Try It

Examine this sample done by an imaginary student named Samuel. Analyze Samuel's work. Cross out unfocused information. What should he do to score higher?

2. How can you use a search engine to search for more information? Use details to support your answer.

   Samuel's Notes: by typing word; search for city, Cheyenne; search Web sites that come up

   Samuel's Answer: You can find out information with a search engine by typing a word. You can find out about the city Cheyenne by typing Cheyenne. You can also search the Web sites that result from using a search engine.

   To score higher, Samuel needs to _____

   _____

Connections Across Continents

Directions: Read this biography. Then follow the directions on pages 16–21.

William Penn: 1644–1718

1   At the age of 22, William Penn, the son of a high-ranking English naval officer, found himself locked in a cell. Earlier that day—September 3, 1667—Penn had been sitting in a quiet room, praying with a group known as the Religious Society of Friends, or "Quakers." The law of England at that time did not allow for a group of Quakers to worship together. Penn and his fellow Quakers believed that they should have the right to pray in the way that felt right to them.

2   Just after the start of the meeting, an English soldier entered the room. Soon more soldiers arrived and arrested everyone present.

3   From his cell, William wrote a letter asking that all the imprisoned Quakers be released. He wrote: "Religion, which is at once my crime and my innocence, makes me a prisoner . . . but mine own free man."

4   Penn and the other Quakers were set free, but Penn would spend much more time in prison because of his religious beliefs. Years later, in 1682, William established Pennsylvania as a new colony in North America. His belief in religious freedom was one of the ideals that guided the new colony. The city of Philadelphia welcomed people of many different backgrounds and religious faiths.

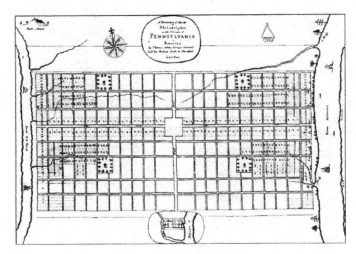

Philadelphia was the first colonial city to be planned on paper before it was built. Penn wanted the city to have wide streets with many trees and green spaces.

Strategy 1 Locate Key Words in the Question

Directions: Before you can answer a question, you need to understand the question. Follow these steps to understand the question.

> * Read the question.
> * Ask yourself: "**Who** or **what** is the question about?" Words that tell "who" or "what" are **key words**. Circle key words.
> * Look for and circle other key words. Often question words and other important words are key words.
> * Turn the question into a statement using key words. Follow this model: "I need to find out ____."

Learn

Read the question. Circle the key words and complete the sentence.

1. (Where) were (Penn) and his (fellow) (Quakers) when they were (arrested)?

   > Circle key words.

   - ⬭ **A** in prison
   - ⬭ **B** in Pennsylvania
   - ⬭ **C** in a quiet room
   - ⬭ **D** in church

   I need to find out _where Penn and his fellow Quakers_

   were when they were arrested.

   > Turn the question into a statement using key words.

Try It

Read each question. Circle the key words and complete each sentence.

2. Why would Penn spend much more time in prison?
   - ⬭ **A** because soldiers did not like him
   - ⬭ **B** because of his religious beliefs
   - ⬭ **C** because he established Pennsylvania
   - ⬭ **D** because his father was a naval officer

   I need to find out _____

   _____

3. What did Penn and his fellow Quakers believe? Use details from the text to support your answer.

   I need to find out _____

   _____

Strategy 2 Locate Key Words in the Text

Directions: You can also understand a question by thinking about where you need to look for the answer. Follow these steps to understand the question.

- Read the question.
- Look for and circle key words in the question.
- Look for and circle key words in the text that match key words in the question.
- Decide where to look for the answer.
  - ➤ To find the answer, you may have to **look in one place in the text**. The answer is *right there* in the text.
  - ➤ To find the answer, you may have to **look in several places in the text**. You have to *think and search* for information.
  - ➤ To find the answer, you may have to **combine what you know with what the author tells you**. The answer comes from *the author and you*.

Learn

Read the question. Circle the key words and complete the sentence.

1. Based on paragraph 4, (when) did (William) (establish) (Pennsylvania)? Use details from the text to support your answer.

   I found the answer in <u>paragraph 4, sentence 2.</u>

> - Look for and circle key words in the question.
> - Look for and circle key words in the text that match key words in the question.

> - The question asks you to find a date.
> - You will have to **look in one place in the text** for information.

Try It

Read each question. Circle the key words and complete each sentence.

2. Based on paragraph 1, what did Penn and his fellow Quakers believe?
   - ◯ A   that religious freedom is not important
   - ◯ B   that they should have the right to pray in their own way
   - ◯ C   that people of other faiths should not be welcomed
   - ◯ D   that they should have the right to make noise in their own room

   I found the answer in _____

   _____

3. How did the arrests of William Penn influence his belief in the religious freedom that guided Pennsylvania? Use details from the text to support your answer.

   I found the answer in _____

   _____

Strategy 3 Choose the Right Answer

Directions: Use this strategy for a multiple-choice question in which you need to choose the best answer. Follow these steps to answer a multiple-choice question.

- Read the question.
- Read each answer choice.
- Rule out any choice you know is wrong. Go back to the text to rule out other choices.
- Mark your answer choice.
- Check your answer by comparing it with the text.

Learn

Cross out any choice you know is wrong. Next, go back to the text to rule out any other choices. Then mark your answer choice.

1. Where were Penn and his fellow Quakers when they were arrested?
   - A ~~in prison~~
   - B ~~in Pennsylvania~~
   - ● C in a quiet room
   - D ~~in church~~

You will have to **look in one place in the text**.

Rule out the incorrect choices. Choose answer C because the text supports this choice.

Try It

Cross out any choice you know is wrong. Next, go back to the text to rule out any other choices. Then mark your answer choice.

2. Why would Penn spend much more time in prison?
   - A because soldiers did not like him
   - B because of his religious beliefs
   - C because he established Pennsylvania
   - D because his father was a naval officer

3. What did Penn and his fellow Quakers believe?
   - A that religious freedom is not important
   - B that they should have the right to pray in their own way
   - C that people of other faiths should not be welcomed
   - D that they should have the right to make noise in their own room

© Scott Foresman 5

Strategy 4 Use Information from the Text

Directions: A question may tell you to support your answer with details from the text. If it does, then you must include information from the text. Follow these steps to answer such questions.

- Read the question.
- Look for and circle key words in the question.
- **Make notes** about details from the text that answer the question.
- Reread the question and your notes.
- If details are missing, go back to the text.

Learn

Use information from the text to answer the question.

1. (Why) was it (dangerous) for a group of (Quakers) to (pray) (together)? Use details from the text to support your answer.

   My Notes: ~~age 22~~, law of England not allow Quakers to pray together, soldiers arrest everyone

   My Answer: The law of England did not allow Quakers to pray together. If they prayed together, Quakers could be arrested.

- Look for and circle key words in the question.
- The question asks for details about why it was dangerous for Quakers to pray together.
- Read the text and **make notes** about why it was dangerous for Quakers to pray together.

Reread the question and cross out any notes that do not apply to the question.

Answer the question in your own words.

Try It

Use information from the text to answer the question.

2. When and where did William Penn establish Pennsylvania? Use details from the text to support your answer.

   My Notes: _____

   _____

   _____

   My Answer: _____

   _____

   _____

   _____

Strategy 5 Use Information from Graphics

Directions: A question may ask you about a map or tell you to support your answer
with details from a map. If it does, then you must include information from the map.
Follow these steps to answer questions about the map.

- Read the question.
- Look for and circle key words in the question.
- Use what you know to analyze the map.
- Use details from the map or facts about the map to
  answer the question.

Learn

Look at the map and read the facts about the map on page 15. Use information from
the map or facts about the map to answer the question.

1. Based on the facts about the map, (what) (city) does the
   (map) (show)? Use details to support your answer.

   | Look for and circle key words in the question. |

   To find the answer, I will *read the facts about the map.*

   | Look at page 15. Analyze the map and the facts about the map. Use details to answer the question. |

   My Answer: *The map shows the city of Philadelphia.*

Try It

Look at the map and read the facts about the map on page 15. Use information from
the map or facts about the map to support your answer.

2. Based on the facts about the map, how was Philadelphia different from the other
   colonial cities? Use details to support your answer.

   To find the answer, I will _____

   _____

   _____

   My Answer: _____

   _____

   _____

   _____

Strategy 6 Write Your Answer to Score High

Directions: A question may tell you to write an answer. Follow these steps to write a correct, complete, and focused answer.

- Read the question.
- Make notes about details that answer the question.
- Reread the question and your notes. If details are missing, go back to the text.
- Begin your answer with words from the question. Include details from your notes.
- Check your answer. Ask yourself:
  - ➤ Is my answer correct? Are some details incorrect?
  - ➤ Is my answer complete? Do I need to add more details?
  - ➤ Is my answer focused? Do all my details help answer the question?

Learn

Examine this sample done by an imaginary student named Maria. Analyze Maria's work. Cross out incorrect information. What should she do to score higher?

1. (Why) was it (dangerous) for a group of (Quakers) to (pray) (together)? Use details from the text to support your answer.

   Maria's Notes: English ~~lawyers~~ not allow Quaker to pray, soldiers arrest everyone

   Maria's Answer: The English lawyers did not allow Quakers to pray. Soldiers arrested them when they prayed.

   > Maria circled key words in the question.

   > Maria's information about lawyers is incorrect.

   > Maria's information about Quakers is incomplete.

   To score higher, Maria needs to replace "lawyers" with "law" to make her answer correct, and add that Quakers were not allowed to pray together to make her answer complete.

Try It

Examine this sample done by an imaginary student named Frank. Analyze Frank's work. Cross out incorrect information. What should he do to score higher?

2. How did the arrests of William Penn influence his belief in the religious freedom that guided Pennsylvania? Use details from the text to support your answer.

   Frank's Notes: spend time in prison for beliefs, established Pennsylvania, belief in political freedom, Philadelphia welcomed people

   Frank's Answer: William was arrested many times. He valued political freedom. He founded Pennsylvania based on this belief. He wanted Philadelphia to welcome all kinds of people.

   To score higher, Frank needs to _____

   _____

© Scott Foresman 5

Colonial Life in North America

Directions: Read about colonial life in North America. Then follow the directions on pages 23–28.

Compare and Contrast Colonial Life in North America

1   As the 13 Colonies grew, they were similar in many ways. All the colonies were ruled by England. All had cities, towns, and farms.

2   But the 13 Colonies also had many differences. The ways of life differed in the three regions. In the New England Colonies, people depended on the sea and the forests. Farms in the region were small. New England had many small towns and some large cities. The Middle Colonies also had small towns and large cities. These colonies produced large amounts of wheat and flour. The Southern Colonies had towns, small farms, and large plantations. Slavery provided the main work force for these plantations.

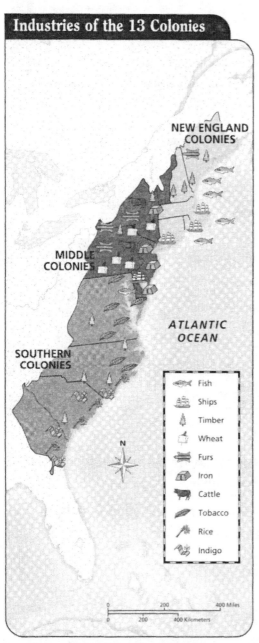

Industries of the 13 Colonies

NEW ENGLAND COLONIES

MIDDLE COLONIES

SOUTHERN COLONIES

ATLANTIC OCEAN

N

Fish
Ships
Timber
Wheat
Furs
Iron
Cattle
Tobacco
Rice
Indigo

0   200   400 Miles
0   200   400 Kilometers

The three colonial regions developed different economies.

Strategy 1 Locate Key Words in the Question

Directions: Before you can answer a question, you need to understand the question. Follow these steps to understand the question.

- Read the question.
- Ask yourself: "**Who** or **what** is the question about?" Words that tell "who" or "what" are **key words**. Circle key words.
- Look for and circle other key words. Often question words and other important words are key words.
- Turn the question into a statement using key words. Follow this model: "I need to find out ____."

Learn

Read the question. Circle the key words and complete the sentence.

1. (How) were the (13 Colonies) (similar)?
   - ⬭ A All were called New England.
   - ⬭ B All had plantations.
   - ⬭ C All had the same way of life.
   - ⬭ D All were ruled by England.

   I need to find out _how the 13 Colonies were similar._

   > Circle key words.

   > Turn the question into a statement using key words.

Try It

Read each question. Circle the key words and complete each sentence.

2. Who depended on the sea and the forests?
   - ⬭ A the people of the New England Colonies
   - ⬭ B the people of the Middle Colonies
   - ⬭ C the people of the Southern Colonies
   - ⬭ D the people of all three regions

   I need to find out _____

   _____

3. Where were large amounts of wheat and flour produced? Use details from the text to support your answer.

   I need to find out _____

   _____

© Scott Foresman 5

Strategy 2 Locate Key Words in the Text

Directions: You can also understand a question by thinking about where you need to look for the answer. Follow these steps to understand the question.

- Read the question.
- Look for and circle key words in the question.
- Look for and circle key words in the text that match key words in the question.
- Decide where to look for the answer.
  - ➤ To find the answer, you may have to **look in one place in the text**. The answer is *right there* in the text.
  - ➤ To find the answer, you may have to **look in several places in the text**. You have to *think and search* for information.
  - ➤ To find the answer, you may have to **combine what you know with what the author tells you**. The answer comes from *the author and you*.

Learn

Read the question. Circle the key words and complete the sentence.

- Look for and circle key words in the question.
- Look for and circle key words in the text that match key words in the question.

1. Based on paragraph 1, (how) were the (13 Colonies) (similar)? Use details from the text to support your answer.

   I found the answer in <u>paragraph 1, sentences 2 and 3.</u>

- The question asks you to tell how the colonies were alike.
- You will have to **look in several places in the text** for information.

Try It

Read each question. Circle the key words and complete each sentence.

2. Based on paragraph 2, where were large amounts of wheat and flour produced?
   - ⬯ **A** in the Middle Colonies
   - ⬯ **B** in the Southern Colonies
   - ⬯ **C** in the New England Colonies
   - ⬯ **D** in all three regions

   I found the answer in _____

_____

3. How were the 13 Colonies similar and different? Use details from the text to support your answer.

   I found the answer in _____

_____

Strategy 3 Choose the Right Answer

Directions: Use this strategy for a multiple-choice question in which you need to choose the best answer. Follow these steps to answer a multiple-choice question.

- Read the question.
- Read each answer choice.
- Rule out any choice you know is wrong. Go back to the text to rule out other choices.
- Mark your answer choice.
- Check your answer by comparing it with the text.

Learn

Cross out any choice you know is wrong. Next, go back to the text to rule out any other choices. Then mark your answer choice.

1. How were the 13 Colonies similar?
   - A ~~all were called New England~~
   - B ~~all had plantations~~
   - C ~~all had the same way of life~~
   - ● D all were ruled by England

You will have to **look in several places in the text**.

Rule out the incorrect choices. Choose answer D because the text supports this choice.

Try It

Cross out any choice you know is wrong. Next, go back to the text to rule out any other choices. Then mark your answer choice.

2. Who depended on the sea and the forests?
   - A the people of the New England Colonies
   - B the people of the Middle Colonies
   - C the people of the Southern Colonies
   - D the people of all three regions

3. Where were large amounts of wheat and flour produced?
   - A in the Middle Colonies
   - B in the Southern Colonies
   - C in the New England Colonies
   - D in all three regions

© Scott Foresman 5

Strategy 4 Use Information from the Text

Directions: A question may tell you to support your answer with details from the text. If it does, then you must include information from the text. Follow these steps to answer such questions.

- Read the question.
- Look for and circle key words in the question.
- **Make notes** about details from the text that answer the question.
- Reread the question and your notes.
- If details are missing, go back to the text.

Learn

Use information from the text to answer the question.

1. (What) did the (people) of the (New England Colonies) (depend) on? Use details from the text to support your answer.

   My Notes: New England Colonies, depended on sea, forests, ~~small towns~~, ~~large cities~~

   My Answer: People in the New England Colonies depended on the sea and forests.

- Look for and circle key words in the question.
- The question asks what things people in the New England Colonies depended on.
- Read the text and **make notes** about what people in the New England Colonies depended on.

Reread the question and cross out any notes that do not apply to the question.

Answer the question in your own words.

Try It

Use information from the text to answer the question.

2. What did the Middle Colonies produce? Use details from the text to support your answer.

   My Notes: _____

   _____

   _____

   My Answer: _____

   _____

   _____

   _____

© Scott Foresman 5

Strategy 5 Use Information from Graphics

Directions: A question may ask you about a map or tell you to support your answer with details from a map. If it does, then you must include information from the map. Follow these steps to answer questions about the map.

- Read the question.
- Look for and circle key words in the question.
- Use what you know to analyze the map.
- Use details from the map to answer the question.

Learn

Look at the map on page 22. Use information from the map to answer the question.

1. Based on the map, (what) (three) (regions) of the 13 Colonies are shown on the (map)? Use details to support your answer.

   > Look for and circle key words in the question.

   To find the answer, I will *look at the labels on the map.*

   My Answer: *The three regions of the 13 Colonies are New England Colonies, Middle Colonies, and Southern Colonies.*

   > Look at page 22. Analyze the map. Use details to answer the question.

Try It

Look at the map on page 22. Use information from the map key to answer the question.

2. What are the three industries identified at the top of the map key? Use details to support your answer.

   To find the answer, I will _____

   _____

   _____

   My Answer: _____

   _____

   _____

   _____

© Scott Foresman 5

Strategy 6 Write Your Answer to Score High

Directions: A question may tell you to write an answer. Follow these steps to write a correct, complete, and focused answer.

- Read the question.
- Make notes about details that answer the question.
- Reread the question and your notes. If details are missing, go back to the text.
- Begin your answer with words from the question. Include details from your notes.
- Check your answer. Ask yourself:
  - ➤ Is my answer correct? Are some details incorrect?
  - ➤ Is my answer complete? Do I need to add more details?
  - ➤ Is my answer focused? Do all my details help answer the question?

Learn

Examine this sample done by an imaginary student named Denis. Analyze Denis's work. Cross out incorrect information. What should he do to score higher?

1. (How) were the (13 Colonies) (similar)? Use details from the text to support your answer.

   | Denis circled key words in the question. |

   Denis's Notes: ruled by ~~New England~~, towns, farms

   | Denis's information about who ruled the 13 Colonies is incorrect. |

   Denis's Answer: The 13 Colonies were similar in many ways. They all were ruled by New England. They all had towns and farms.

   | Denis's notes are incomplete. |

   To score higher, Denis needs to replace "New England" with "England" and add that the

   13 Colonies all had cities.

Try It

Examine this sample done by an imaginary student named Dexter. Analyze Dexter's work. Cross out incorrect information. What should he do to score higher?

2. How were the 13 Colonies different? Use details from the text to support your answer.

   Dexter's Notes: ways of life; New England, sea, forests; Middle, wheat; Southern, plants

   Dexter's Answer: The 13 Colonies were very different. The New England Colonies depended on the sea and forests. The Middle Colonies produced wheat. The Southern Colonies had large plants.

   To score higher, Dexter needs to _____

   _____

The American Revolution

Directions: Read this biography. Then follow the directions on pages 30–35.

Phillis Wheatley: about 1753–1784

1   Phillis Wheatley was seven years old when she was kidnapped from her home in West Africa. She was shipped to Boston and sold as a slave to the wealthy Wheatley family.

2   The Wheatley family realized that Phillis was extremely intelligent. They encouraged her to study, which very few slaves were allowed to do. In 1773, she became the first African American to have a book of poetry published. That same year Phillis was released from slavery.

3   Now famous throughout New England for her writing, she became a strong supporter of the colonists' struggle for freedom from Britain. In 1775, she wrote a poem about General George Washington. He liked the poem so much that he invited Wheatley to come visit him.

4   Phillis Wheatley also spoke out against slavery. She wrote: "In every human . . . God has implanted a principle, which we call love of freedom."

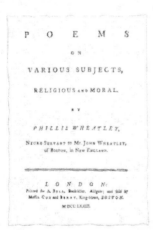

Wheatley's book contained a letter that declared she was the actual author of the poems. It was signed by 18 important Boston citizens.

Strategy 1 Locate Key Words in the Question

Learn

Read the question. Circle the key words and complete the sentence.

1. (Where) was (Phillis Wheatley's) (first) (home)?

   ⊂⊃ **A** Boston
   ⊂⊃ **B** West Africa
   ⊂⊃ **C** Washington, D.C.
   ⊂⊃ **D** London

   I need to find out *where Phillis Wheatley's first home was.* _____

> Circle key words.

> Turn the question into a statement using key words.

Try It

Read each question. Circle the key words and complete each sentence.

2. Based on paragraph 2, who realized that Phillis was extremely intelligent?

   ⊂⊃ **A** slaves
   ⊂⊃ **B** her parents
   ⊂⊃ **C** the Wheatley family
   ⊂⊃ **D** poets

   I need to find out _____

   _____

   _____

3. Why did Phillis Wheatley become famous throughout New England? Use details from the text to support your answer.

   I need to find out _____

   _____

   _____

4. Why might Phillis Wheatley have become a strong supporter of the colonists' struggle for freedom? Use details from the text to support your answer.

   I need to find out _____

   _____

   _____

© Scott Foresman 5

Strategy 2 Locate Key Words in the Text

Learn

Read the question. Circle the key words and complete the sentence.

> • Look for and circle key words in the question.
> • Look for and circle key words in the text that match key words in the question.

1. (Why) did Phillis (Wheatley) become (famous) throughout (New England?) Use details from the text to support your answer.

   I found the answer in _paragraph 2, sentence 3; paragraph_

   3, sentence 1; and what I already know. _____

> • The question asks you to compare Phillis Wheatley's trips.
> • You will have to **combine what you know with what the author tells you.**

Try It

Read each question. Circle the key words and complete each sentence.

2. Where was Phillis Wheatley's first home? Use details from the text to support your answer.

   ⬭ **A** London

   ⬭ **B** Boston

   ⬭ **C** West Africa

   ⬭ **D** Washington, D.C.

   I found the answer in _____

   _____

   _____

3. Why might Phillis Wheatley have become a strong supporter of the colonists' struggle for freedom? Use details from the text to support your answer.

   I found the answer in _____

   _____

   _____

4. How was Phillis Wheatley's life different from that of other slaves?

   I found the answer in _____

   _____

   _____

Strategy 3 Choose the Right Answer

Learn

Cross out any choice you know is wrong. Next, go back to the text to rule out any other choices. Then mark your answer choice.

1. Where was Phillis Wheatley's first home?
   - ⬭ A ~~London~~
   - ⬭ B ~~Boston~~
   - ⬤ C West Africa
   - ⬭ D ~~Washington, D.C.~~

> You will have to **look in one place in the text**.

> Rule out the incorrect choices. Choose answer C because the text supports this choice.

Try It

Cross out any choice you know is wrong. Next, go back to the text to rule out any other choices. Then mark your answer choice.

2. Who realized that Phillis was extremely intelligent?
   - ⬭ A slaves
   - ⬭ B her parents
   - ⬭ C poets
   - ⬭ D the Wheatley family

3. Why did Phillis become famous throughout New England?
   - ⬭ A She was the first African American to have a book of poetry published.
   - ⬭ B she had been kidnapped in Africa
   - ⬭ C she belonged to a wealthy family
   - ⬭ D she was encouraged to study

4. Why might Phillis Wheatley have become a strong supporter of the colonists' struggle for freedom?
   - ⬭ A She wanted Washington to be King of America.
   - ⬭ B She understood the importance of freedom.
   - ⬭ C She was angry at the English because they did not buy her book.
   - ⬭ D She believed it would release the Wheatley family from slavery.

© Scott Foresman 5

Strategy 4 Use Information from the Text

Learn

Use information from the text to answer the question.

1. Based on paragraph 1, (where) was (Phillis Wheatley's) (first) (home)? Use details from the text to support your answer.

My Notes: Phillis Wheatley, first home, West Africa, ~~shipped to Boston~~

My Answer: Phillis Wheatley's first home was in West Africa.

- Look for and circle key words in the question.
- The question asks for a location.
- Read the text and **make notes** about where Phillis Wheatley's home was.

Reread the question and cross any notes that do not apply to the question.

Answer the question in your own words.

Try It

Use information from the text to answer each question.

2. Based on paragraph 2, who realized that Phillis was extremely intelligent? Use details from the text to support your answer.

My Notes: _____

_____

_____

My Answer: _____

_____

_____

3. Based on paragraph 3, why did George Washington invite Phillis Wheatley to visit him? Use details from the text to support your answer.

My Notes: _____

_____

_____

My Answer: _____

_____

_____

Strategy 5 Use Information from Graphics

Learn

Look at the photograph of the book cover on page 29. Use the photograph to answer the question.

1. Based on the photograph, who was the author of the book? Use details to support your answer.

   To find the answer, I will look at the top of the book

   cover.

   My Answer: The author of the book was Phillis

   Wheatley.

> Look for and circle key words in the question.

> Look at page 29. Analyze the photograph of the book. Use details to answer the question.

Try It

Look at the photograph of the book cover on page 29. Use information from the photograph to answer each question.

2. Based on the photograph, where was the book published? Use details to support your answer.

   To find the answer, I will _____

   _____

   _____

   My Answer: _____

   _____

   _____

3. Based on the photograph, what was the full title of the book? Use details to support your answer.

   To find the answer, I will _____

   _____

   _____

   My Answer: _____

   _____

   _____

© Scott Foresman 5

Strategy 6 Write Your Answer to Score High

Learn

Examine this sample done by an imaginary student named Mario. Analyze Mario's work. Cross out incorrect information. What should he do to score higher?

1. (What) (happened) to (Phillis) right after she was (kidnapped) from her home in West Africa? Use details from the text to support your answer.

   | Mario circled key words in the question. |

   Mario's Notes: kidnapped, home in West Africa, shipped to Boston, ended up with ~~Wheat~~ family

   | Mario's notes are incomplete. |

   Mario's Answer: After Phillis was kidnapped from her home in West Africa, she was sent to Boston. She ending up living with a family named Wheat.

   | Mario's information about the name of the family is incorrect. |

   To score higher, Mario needs to replace "Wheat" with "Wheatley" and add that Phillis was

   sold to the Wheatley family.

Try It

Examine this sample done by an imaginary student named Judith. Analyze Judith's work. Cross out incorrect information. What should she do to score higher?

2. What were the differences between Phillis and the Wheatley family? Use details from the text to support your answer.

   Judith's Notes: Phillis, African, encouraged to study, poet; Wheatley family, healthy

   Judith's Answer: Phillis was African. It was special for her to study. She was a poet. The Wheatley family was healthy.

   To score higher, Judith needs to _____

   _____

   _____

   _____

Life in a New Nation

Directions: Read this biography. Then follow the directions on pages 37–42.

Benjamin Banneker: 1731–1806

1   When Benjamin Banneker was about 21, he saw a pocket watch that belonged to a man named Josef Levi. Banneker was fascinated by the watch. Levi gave it to him, and Banneker took it apart to see how it worked. He studied the pieces and used them as a model to create a clock made entirely out of wood.

2   Years later Banneker's attention to detail helped save the plan for the nation's new capital city. In 1790, Banneker was placed on the surveying team for the capital at Thomas Jefferson's request. When Pierre L'Enfant, the head designer, suddenly quit, he took the city plans with him. Banneker was able to re-create the work from memory in a few days, saving the project from a serious setback.

3   Banneker made use of his growing fame to speak out against slavery. Although Banneker grew up free on his family's farm in Maryland, his father had been a slave and he knew the effects of slavery.

4   When Banneker completed his first book, he sent it to Secretary of State Thomas Jefferson and included a note asking Jefferson to help improve the treatment of African Americans. He wrote: "However variable [different] we may be in society or religion, however diversified in situation or color, we are all in the same family and stand in the same relation to [God]."

Designing Washington, D.C.

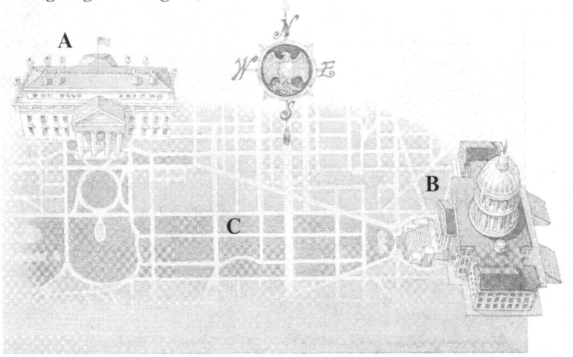

Strategy 1 Locate Key Words in the Question

Learn

Read the question. Circle the key words and complete the sentence.

1. (What) did (Banneker) (take) (apart) to see how it worked?

        Circle key words.

   ⬭ **A**   the plan for the nation's new capital city
   ⬭ **B**   his family's farm
   ⬭ **C**   a clock
   ⬭ **D**   a pocket watch

   I need to find out _what Banneker took apart to see_

   how it worked.

        Turn the question into a statement using key words.

Try It

Read each question. Circle the key words and complete each sentence.

2. How was Banneker able to re-create the city plans?

   ⬭ **A**   by copying them by hand
   ⬭ **B**   by photocopying them
   ⬭ **C**   by remembering them
   ⬭ **D**   by asking the head designer to describe them

   I need to find out _____

   _____

   _____

3. How did Banneker make use of his growing fame? Use details from the text to support your answer.

   I need to find out _____

   _____

   _____

4. What did Banneker ask Jefferson to do? Use details from the text to support your answer.

   I need to find out _____

   _____

   _____

Strategy 2 **Locate Key Words in the Text**

Learn

Read the question. Circle the key words and complete
the sentence.

- Look for and circle key words in the question.
- Look for and circle key words in the text that match key words in the question.

1. What did Banneker's (attention) to (detail) (enable)
   him (to) (do) ? Use details from the text to support
   your answer.

   I found the answer in paragraph 1, sentence 4, and

   paragraph 2, sentences 1 and 4.

- The question asks you to find examples of what Banneker's attention to detail enabled him to do.
- You will have to **look in several places in the text** for information.

Try It

Read each question. Circle the key words and complete each
sentence.

2. How was Banneker able to re-create the city plans?
   - ⬭ **A** by copying them by hand
   - ⬭ **B** by photocopying them
   - ⬭ **C** by remembering them
   - ⬭ **D** by asking the head designer to describe them

   I found the answer in _____

   _____

   _____

3. What were two ways that Banneker helped others? Use details from the text
   to support your answer.

   I found the answer in _____

   _____

   _____

4. What did Banneker ask Jefferson to do? Use details from the text to support
   your answer.

   I found the answer in _____

   _____

   _____

Strategy 3 Choose the Right Answer

Learn

Cross out any choice you know is wrong. Next, go back to the text to rule out any other choices. Then mark your answer choice.

1. What did Banneker take apart to see how it worked?

  ○ A ~~the plan for the nation's new capital city~~
  ○ B ~~his family's farm~~
  ○ C ~~a clock~~
  ● D a pocket watch

> You will have to **look in one place in the text**.

> Rule out the incorrect choices. Choose answer D because the text supports this choice.

Try It

Cross out any choice you know is wrong. Next, go back to the text to rule out any other choices. Then mark your answer choice.

2. How was Banneker able to re-create the city plans?

  ○ A by copying them by hand
  ○ B by photocopying them
  ○ C by remembering them
  ○ D by asking the head designer to describe them

3. How did Banneker make use of his growing fame?

  ○ A by signing autographs
  ○ B by speaking out against slavery
  ○ C by quitting his job
  ○ D by endorsing products

4. What did Banneker ask Jefferson to do?

  ○ A visit his family farm
  ○ B let him design a new city
  ○ C help improve the treatment of African Americans
  ○ D give him a job

© Scott Foresman 5

Strategy 4 Use Information from the Text

Learn

Use information from the text to answer the question.

1. Based on paragraph 1, (what) did (Banneker) (take) (apart) to see how it worked? Use details from the text to support your answer.

   My Notes: pocket watch, Banneker, took apart, see how worked, ~~used pieces to create clock~~

   My Answer: Banneker took apart a pocket watch to see how it worked.

- Look for and circle key words in the question.
- The question asks you to identify the thing that Banneker took apart.
- Read the text and **make notes** about what Banneker took apart.

Reread the question and cross out any notes that do not apply to the question.

Answer the question in your own words.

Try It

Use information from the text to answer each question.

2. Based on paragraph 3, where did Banneker grow up? Use details from the text to support your answer.

   My Notes: _____

   _____

   _____

   My Answer: _____

   _____

   _____

3. On what did Banneker base his belief in equality? Use details from the text to support your answer.

   My Notes: _____

   _____

   _____

   My Answer: _____

   _____

   _____

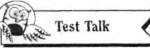
Strategy 5 Use Information from Graphics

Learn

Look at the map on page 36. Use information from the map to answer the question.

1. The White House has a roofed porch with four columns at the entrance. Based on the map, (what) (letter) marks the (White House)? Use details to support your answer.

   > Look for and circle key words in the question.

   To find the answer, I will look for the letter near

   the White House.

   > Look at the map on page 36. Analyze the map. Use details to answer the question.

   My Answer: The letter A marks the White House.

Try It

Look at the map and compass rose on page 36. Use information from the map and compass rose to answer each question.

2. The Capitol has a large dome. Based on the map and compass rose, is the White House to the east or the west of the Capitol? Use details to support your answer.

   To find the answer, I will _____

   _____

   _____

   My Answer: _____

   _____

   _____

3. Based on the map and compass rose, is the White House north or south of the Capitol? Use details to support your answer.

   To find the answer, I will _____

   _____

   _____

   My Answer: _____

   _____

   _____

Strategy 6 Write Your Answer to Score High

Learn

Examine this sample done by an imaginary student named Mary. Analyze Mary's work. Cross out incorrect or unfocused information. What should she do to score higher?

1. (How) was (Banneker) able to (create) a (clock) out of (wood)? Use details from the text to support your answer.

Mary circled key words in the question.

   Mary's Notes: ~~Banneker about 21~~, pocket watch, take apart, studied plans, used them as model, create clock out of wood

Mary's notes include unfocused information.

Mary's notes are incorrect.

   Mary's Answer: Banneker was about 21 years old and he was able to create a clock out of wood because he took apart a pocket watch, studied the plans and used them as a model.

   To score higher, Mary needs to _replace "plans" with "pieces" and cross out unfocused_

   information about Banneker's age to make her answer correct and focused.

Try It

Examine this sample done by an imaginary student named Eric. Analyze Eric's work. Cross out incorrect or unfocused information. What should he do to score higher?

2. What did Banneker do to help African Americans? Use details from the text to support your answer.

   Eric's Notes: Banneker grew up free, speak out for slavery, sent first book to Secretary Thomas Jefferson, note, asked Jefferson to help African Americans

   Eric's Answer: Benjamin Banneker grew up free. He spoke out for slavery. He sent his first book to Secretary Thomas Jefferson. He also sent a note. The note asked Jefferson to help African Americans.

   To score higher, Eric needs to _____

   _____

   _____

   _____

   _____

A Growing Nation

Directions: Read about a cross-section diagram. Then follow the directions on pages 44–49.

Read a Cross-Section Diagram

1   To use a cross-section diagram, you have to study the drawing carefully. Read the labels to identify each part of the diagram.

2   The diagram on this page shows how a boat moves from higher to lower water in the lock of a canal. A lock is a section of a canal that is closed off so that water can be removed or added. The water coming in or going out changes the level of the water in the lock so that a boat can be moved higher or lower.

3   Look at the cross-section diagram. Notice that the boat has to be moved to a lower water level.

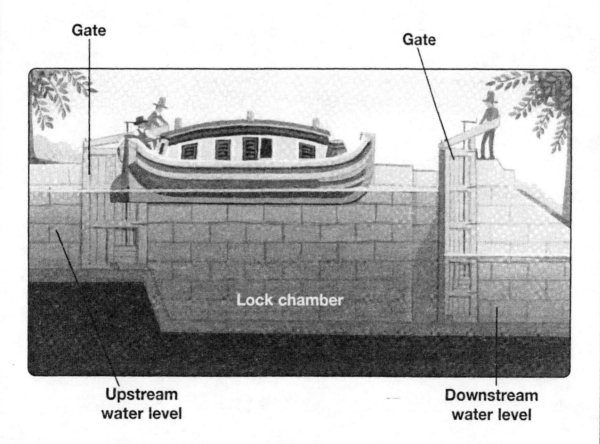

Gate

Gate

Lock chamber

Upstream water level

Downstream water level

Strategy 1 Locate Key Words in the Question

Learn

Read the question. Circle the key words and complete the sentence.

1. Based on paragraph 1, (how) can you (identify) (each) (part)
   of a (diagram)?

   | Circle key words. |

   ⬭ **A** Read the labels.
   ⬭ **B** Look at the drawing closely.
   ⬭ **C** Ride a boat through a canal.
   ⬭ **D** Add labels.

   I need to find out _how I can identify each part of_

   a diagram.

   | Turn the question into a statement using key words. |

Try It

Read each question. Circle the key words and complete each sentence.

2. What is a lock?

   ⬭ **A** a kind of diagram
   ⬭ **B** a section of a canal that is closed off
   ⬭ **C** a level of water in a canal
   ⬭ **D** a gate

   I need to find out _____

   _____

   _____

3. Why does the level of the water in the lock need to be changed? Use details
   from the text to support your answer.

   I need to find out _____

   _____

   _____

4. Based on paragraph 3, where is the boat being moved to? Use details from the text
   to support your answer.

   I need to find out _____

   _____

   _____

Strategy 2 Find Key Words in the Text

Learn

Read the question. Circle the key words and complete the sentence.

1. Based on paragraph 1, (how) can you (identify) (each) (part) of a (diagram)? Use details from the text to support your answer.

   I found the answer in paragraph 1, sentence 2.

> • Look for and circle key words in the question.
> • Look for and circle key words in the text that match key words in the question.

> • The question asks you how you can identify each part of the diagram.
> • You will have to **look in one place in the text** for information.

Try It

Read each question. Circle the key words and complete each sentence.

2. Based on paragraph 2, what is a lock?
   - ⬭ **A** a kind of diagram
   - ⬭ **B** a section of a canal that is closed off
   - ⬭ **C** a level of water in a canal
   - ⬭ **D** a gate

   I found the answer in _____

   _____

   _____

3. Why does the level of the water in the lock need to be changed? Use details from the text to support your answer.

   I found the answer in _____

   _____

   _____

4. Based on paragraph 3, where is the boat being moved to? Use details from the text to support your answer.

   I found the answer in _____

   _____

   _____

Strategy 3 Choose the Right Answer

Learn

Cross out any choice you know is wrong. Next, go back to the text to rule out any other choices. Then mark your answer choice.

1. Based on paragraph 1, how can you identify each part of a diagram?

   ● **A** Read the labels.
   ○ **B** ~~Look at the drawing closely.~~
   ○ **C** ~~Ride a boat through a canal.~~
   ○ **D** ~~Add labels.~~

> You will have to **look in one place in the text**.

> Rule out the incorrect choices. Choose answer A because the text supports this choice.

Try It

Cross out any choice you know is wrong. Next, go back to the text to rule out any other choices. Then mark your answer choice.

2. What is a lock?

   ○ **A** a kind of diagram
   ○ **B** a section of a canal that is closed off
   ○ **C** a level of water in a canal
   ○ **D** a gate

3. Why does the level of the water in the lock need to be changed?

   ○ **A** so the boat can be moved higher or lower
   ○ **B** so the boat can be cleaned
   ○ **C** so the water can be cleaned
   ○ **D** so the boat is locked in

4. Based on paragraph 3, where is the boat being moved to?

   ○ **A** to a lower water level
   ○ **B** to a higher water level
   ○ **C** to dry dock
   ○ **D** to a river

Strategy 4 Use Information from the Text

Learn

Use information from the text to answer the question.

- Look for and circle key words in the question.
- The question asks how to identify each part of a diagram.
- Read the text and **make notes** about how to identify each part of a diagram.

1. Based on paragraph 1, (how) can you (identify) (each) (part) of a (diagram)?

   My Notes: labels, identify, each part, diagram, ~~upstream water level, downstream water level, gates~~

   My Answer: You can identify each part of a diagram by reading the labels.

Reread the question and cross out any notes that do not apply to the question.

Answer the question in your own words.

Try It

Use information from the text to answer each question.

2. Why does the level of the water in the lock need to be changed? Use details from the text to support your answer.

   My Notes: _____

   _____

   _____

   My Answer: _____

   _____

   _____

   _____

3. What keeps the boat in the lock? Use details from the text to support your answer.

   My Notes: _____

   _____

   _____

   My Answer: _____

   _____

   _____

   _____

Strategy 5 Use Information from Graphics

Learn

Look at the parts of the diagram on page 43 and read the labels. Use information from the diagram to answer the question.

1. Based on the diagram, (what) is the (area) (between) the two (gates) (called)?

   > Look for and circle key words in the question.

   To find the answer, I will <u>look closely at the parts of</u>

   <u>the diagram and read the labels.</u>

   My Answer: <u>The area between the two gates is called</u>

   <u>the lock chamber.</u>

   > Look at page 43. Analyze the diagram. Use details to answer the question.

Try It

Look at the diagram on page 43. Use information from the diagram to answer each question.

2. Based on the diagram, what keeps a boat in a lock chamber? Use details to support your answer.

   To find the answer, I will _____

   _____

   _____

   My Answer: _____

   _____

   _____

3. Based on the diagram, is the boat moving to the upstream water level or the downstream water level? Use details to support your answer.

   To find the answer, I will _____

   _____

   _____

   My Answer: _____

   _____

   _____

Strategy 6 Write Your Answer to Score High

Learn

Examine this sample done by an imaginary student named Carla. Analyze Carla's work. Cross out incorrect or unfocused information. What should she do to score higher?

1. (How) do you (use) a (cross-section diagram)? Use details from the text to support your answer.

   Carla's Notes: study drawing carefully, ~~make~~ labels to identify parts, ~~upstream water level, downstream level, gates~~

   Carla's Answer: When you use a cross-section diagram, you have to study the drawing carefully. You also have to make labels that identify the parts of the diagram. The labels on this diagram are "upstream water level," "downstream water level," and "gate" used twice.

   To score higher, Carla needs to replace "make labels" with "read labels," and cross out the unfocused information about the different parts of the diagram.

   > Carla circled key words in the question.

   > Carla's notes are incorrect.

   > Carla's information about how to use a cross-section diagram is unfocused.

Try It

Examine this sample done by an imaginary student named Paul. Analyze Paul's work. Cross out incorrect or unfocused information. What should he do to score higher?

2. Why does the level of the water in the lock need to be changed? Use details from the text to support your answer.

   Paul's Notes: water coming in or going out changes level of water in stream; so boat can be moved higher or lower; boat moved lower

   Paul's Answer: The level of the water needs to be changed. That way the boat can be moved higher or lower in the stream. In this case, the boat is moved lower.

   To score higher, Paul needs to _____

   _____
   _____
   _____
   _____

War Divides the Nation

Directions: Read this biography. Then follow the directions on pages 51–56.

Robert E. Lee: 1807–1870

1   Robert E. Lee lost his father at an early age. When Robert was six, his father, Harry Lee, visited a friend who published a newspaper that criticized the United States for going to war with Britain in 1812. Like his friend, Harry Lee opposed this war. A group of angry people attacked the newspaper offices while Harry Lee was inside, and he was badly beaten. Robert had to say goodbye as his father boarded a ship to Barbados, where he went to heal from his wounds. Harry Lee died before he could return home.

2   Many years later, at the beginning of the Civil War, Robert E. Lee was asked to make the most difficult decision of his life. Lee was a rising star in the United States Army. But Lee had been born and raised in Virginia, and, although he personally disapproved of slavery, he loved his home and his state. Perhaps he thought of his father, who had defended the things he loved at great cost to himself. Lee resigned from the United States Army, and wrote: "I have not been able to make up my mind to raise my hand against my relatives, my children, my home."

3   Lee hoped that Virginia would not take sides in the conflict, and he would not have to fight at all. But when Virginia seceded and joined the Confederacy, his path became clear to him. Lee accepted a position commanding Virginia's armies. Later, Lee's wife Mary remembered the night of his decision. She said that he had "wept tears of blood."

The Union and the Confederacy, 1861-1865

Legend:
- Union states
- Confederate states
- Border states
- Union-held territories

© Scott Foresman 5

Strategy 1 **Locate Key Words in the Question**

Learn

Read the question. Circle the key words and complete the sentence.

1. (Where) had Robert E. (Lee) been (born) and (raised)?

   | Circle key words. |

   - ⬭ **A** on a star
   - ⬭ **B** in Virginia
   - ⬭ **C** in the United States Army
   - ⬭ **D** in Barbados

   I need to find out <u>where Robert E. Lee was born and</u>

   <u>raised.</u>

   | Turn the question into a statement using key words. |

Try It

Read each question. Circle the key words and complete each sentence.

2. Based on paragraph 2, what did Lee love?
   - ⬭ **A** slavery
   - ⬭ **B** fighting
   - ⬭ **C** vacationing in Barbados
   - ⬭ **D** his home and his state

   I need to find out _____

   _____

   _____

3. When did Lee's path become clear to him? Use details from the text to support your answer.

   I need to find out _____

   _____

   _____

4. What difficult decision did Lee make? Use details from the text to support your answer.

   I need to find out _____

   _____

   _____

Strategy 2 **Locate Key Words in the Text**

Learn

Read the question. Circle the key words and complete
the sentence.

- Look for and circle key words in the question.
- Look for and circle key words in the text that match key words in the question.

1. Based on paragraph 2, (what) (made) (Lee's)
   (decision) so (difficult)? Use details from the
   text to support your answer.

   I found the answer in _paragraph 2, sentences 3–5._

- The question asks you for the details that explain what made Lee's decision so difficult.
- You will have to **look in several places in the text** for information.

Try It

Read each question. Circle the key words and complete each sentence.

2. Based on paragraphs 2 and 3, why did Lee accept a position commanding
   Virginia's forces?

       ◯ **A** He approved of slavery.

       ◯ **B** He believed he had to fight for his state.

       ◯ **C** He hated the United States.

       ◯ **D** He disapproved of slavery.

   I found the answer in _____

   _____

   _____

3. What armies did Lee join? Use details from the text to support your answer.

   I found the answer in _____

   _____

   _____

4. What difficult decision did Lee make? Use details from the text to support
   your answer.

   I found the answer in _____

   _____

   _____

Strategy 3 Choose the Right Answer

Learn

Cross out any choice you know is wrong. Next, go back to the text to rule out any other choices. Then mark your answer choice.

1. Where had Robert E. Lee been born and raised?

    ⬭ **A** ~~on a star~~

    ⬤ **B** in Virginia

    ⬭ **C** ~~in the United States Army~~

    ⬭ **D** ~~in Barbados~~

> You will have to **look in one place in the text**.

> Rule out the incorrect choices. Choose answer B because the text supports this choice.

Try It

Cross out any choice you know is wrong. Next, go back to the text to rule out any other choices. Then mark your answer choice.

2. Based on paragraph 2, where was Lee a rising star?

    ⬭ **A** in the Confederate Army

    ⬭ **B** in the movies

    ⬭ **C** in a large company in Virginia

    ⬭ **D** in the United States Army

3. Based on paragraph 2, what did Lee love?

    ⬭ **A** slavery

    ⬭ **B** fighting

    ⬭ **C** vacationing in Barbados

    ⬭ **D** his home and his state

4. Why did Lee accept a position commanding Virginia's forces?

    ⬭ **A** He approved of slavery.

    ⬭ **B** He believed he had to fight for his state.

    ⬭ **C** He hated the United States.

    ⬭ **D** He disapproved of slavery.

Strategy 4 Use Information from the Text

Learn

Use information from the text to answer the question.

1. Based on paragraph 2, (what) did (Lee) (love)? Use details from the text to support your answer.

   My Notes: Lee, ~~disapproved~~, ~~slavery~~, loved, his home, his state

   My Answer: Lee loved his home and his state.

- Look for and circle key words in the question.
- The question asks not "who" but "what" Lee loved.
- Read the text and **make notes** about what Lee loved.

Reread the question and cross out any notes that do not apply to the question.

Answer the question in your own words.

Try It

Use information from the text to answer each question.

2. Why did Lee resign from the United States Army? Use details from the text to support your answer.

   My Notes: _____

   _____

   _____

   My Answer: _____

   _____

   _____

   _____

3. When did Lee's path become clear to him? Use details from the text to support your answer.

   My Notes: _____

   _____

   _____

   My Answer: _____

   _____

   _____

   _____

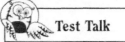
Strategy 5 Use Information from Graphics

Learn

Look at the map on page 50. Use information from the map to answer the question.

1. (What) (explanations) are listed (in) the (map) (key)? Use details to support your answer.

> Look for and circle key words in the question.

   To find the answer, I will *read the list of explanations* *in the map key.*

   My Answer: *The explanations in the map key are* *"Union states," "Confederate states," "Border states,"* *and "Union-held territories."*

> Look at page 50. Analyze the map. Use details to answer the question.

Try It

Look at the map on page 50. Use the information from the map to answer each question.

2. Based on the map, how many states were in the Confederacy? Use details to support your answer.

   To find the answer, I will _____

   _____

   _____

   My Answer: _____

   _____

   _____

3. Based on the map, was the Confederacy in the east, west, north, or south of the United States? Use details to support your answer.

   To find the answer, I will _____

   _____

   _____

   My Answer: _____

   _____

   _____

Test Talk

Use with Unit 7.

Strategy 6 Write Your Answer to Score High

Learn

Examine this sample done by an imaginary student named Lance. Analyze Lance's work.
Cross out incorrect or unfocused information. What should he do to score higher?

1. Based on paragraph 3, (what) did (Lee) (hope)? Use details
   from the text to support your answer.

   | Lance circled key words in the question. |

   Lance's Notes: Lee hoped Virginia ~~take sides~~, not want
   to fight, ~~Virginia seceded~~, ~~path clear~~

   | Lance's information about Virginia taking sides is incorrect. |

   Lance's Answer: Lee hoped that Virginia would
   take sides. He did not want to fight. When Virginia left
   the United States, he knew what he had to do.

   | Lance's notes are unfocused. |

   To score higher, Lance needs to say that Lee hoped Virginia would not take sides, and

   cross out unfocused information about when Lee's path became clear.

Try It

Examine this sample done by an imaginary student named Amina. Analyze Amina's work.
Cross out incorrect or unfocused information. What should she do to score higher?

2. Why did Lee accept a position commanding Virginia's forces? Use details from the
   text to explain your answer.

   Amina's Notes: Lee loved Virginia, Virginia succeeded, joined Confederacy, accepted
   position commanding Virginia's forces, wife Mary remembered decision

   Amina's Answer: Lee accepted a position commanding Virginia's forces because he
   loved Virginia. When Virginia succeeded and joined the Confederacy, he believed he had to
   fight for his state. His wife remembered his decision.

   To score higher, Amina needs to _____

   _____

   _____

   _____

   _____

Expansion and Change

Directions: Read this biography. Then follow the directions on pages 58–63.

Mary Antin: 1881–1949

1   Thirteen-year-old Mary Antin could not believe her eyes. After years of waiting and hoping, her mother finally had ship tickets to take the whole family to the United States. Mary's father had sent the tickets. He had gone to Boston, Massachusetts, to find work three years earlier. Mary's family was Jewish, and because of their religion they were denied many rights in their homeland of Russia. There was always the danger of pogroms, or organized attacks against Jews. Mary's father believed that they would all have better lives in the United States.

2   Before Mary left for the United States, her uncle made her promise that she would write down everything about her journey. Just to reach the ship was difficult, and

Mary was often scared. She sometimes traveled in trains so crowded that there was no room to move.

3   Finally, Mary boarded a ship to cross the Atlantic Ocean. She later described the end of her journey: "And so suffering, fearing, brooding, rejoicing, we crept nearer and nearer to the coveted [desired] shore, until, on a glorious May morning, six weeks after our departure from [Russia], our eyes beheld the Promised Land, and my father received us in his arms."

4   Mary kept her promise to her uncle and wrote a long letter about the trip that brought her to a new land. Later, she would use a copy of this letter as a basis for several successful books about her experiences.

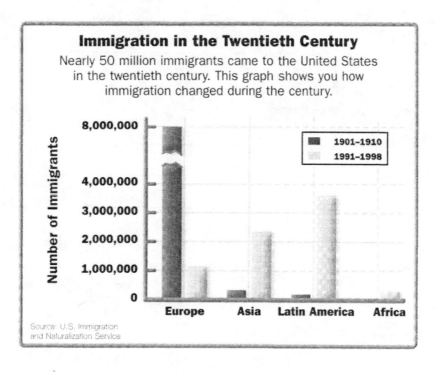

Immigration in the Twentieth Century

Nearly 50 million immigrants came to the United States in the twentieth century. This graph shows you how immigration changed during the century.

Legend: ■ 1901–1910   ▨ 1991–1998

Y-axis: Number of Immigrants (0, 1,000,000, 2,000,000, 3,000,000, 4,000,000, 8,000,000)

X-axis: Europe, Asia, Latin America, Africa

Source: U.S. Immigration and Naturalization Service

Strategy 1 Locate Key Words in the Question

Learn

Read the question. Circle the key words and complete the sentence.

1. (What) is a (pogrom)?

   - ◯ **A** an organized attack against Jews
   - ◯ **B** a Russian political party during the 1800s
   - ◯ **C** a celebration held by Jewish people
   - ◯ **D** a branch of the military in Russia

   I need to find out _what a pogrom is._

> Circle key words.

> Turn the question into a statement using key words.

Try It

Read each question. Circle the key words and complete each sentence.

2. In about what year did Mary leave Russia?

   - ◯ **A** 1881
   - ◯ **B** 1894
   - ◯ **C** 1949
   - ◯ **D** 1936

   I need to find out _____

   _____

   _____

3. Based on paragaraph 1, why was life in Russia hard for Jewish families? Use details from the text to support your answer.

   I need to find out _____

   _____

   _____

4. Based on paragaraph 3, what were the feelings of some of the passengers on the ship? Use details from the text to support your answer.

   I need to find out _____

   _____

   _____

© Scott Foresman 5

Strategy 2 Locate Key Words in the Text

Learn

Read the question. Circle the key words and complete
the sentence.

1. Based on paragraph 1, (why) was (life) in Russia (hard) for
   (Jewish families)? Use details from the text to support
   your answer.

   I found the answer in <u>paragraph 1, sentences 5 and 6.</u>

- Look for and circle key words in the question.
- Look for and circle key words in the text that match key words in the question.

- The question asks you to find details that give reasons why life was hard.
- You will have to **look in several places in the text** for information.

Try It

Read each question. Circle the key words and complete each sentence.

2. Based on the dates in the title, in what year was Mary Antin born?

   ⬭ **A** 1881
   ⬭ **B** 1891
   ⬭ **C** 1894
   ⬭ **D** 1949

   I found the answer in _____

   _____

   _____

3. Based on paragraph 3, what were the feelings of some of the passengers on
   the ship? Use details from the text to support your answer.

   I found the answer in _____

   _____

   _____

4. Based on paragraph 4, how did the letter to her uncle influence Mary's own
   life? Use details from the text to support your answer.

   I found the answer in _____

   _____

   _____

Strategy 3 Choose the Right Answer

Learn

Cross out any choice you know is wrong. Next, go back to the text to rule out
any other choices. Then mark your answer choice.

1. Before Mary left for the United States, what did her
   uncle make her promise to do?

   ⊂⊃ A ~~send him a ship ticket~~

   ⊂⊃ B ~~return to Russia in one year~~

   ⬤ C write about her journey

   ⊂⊃ D ~~work hard in America~~

> You will have to **look in one place in the text**.

> Rule out the incorrect choices. Choose answer C because the text supports this choice.

Try It

Cross out any choice you know is wrong. Next, go back to the text to rule out any
other choices. Then mark your answer choice.

2. Based on paragraph 1, why was life in Russia hard for Jewish families?

   ⊂⊃ A They were denied many rights.

   ⊂⊃ B They did not speak Russian.

   ⊂⊃ C They were not allowed on trains.

   ⊂⊃ D They could not write letters.

3. What is a pogrom?

   ⊂⊃ A something one desires

   ⊂⊃ B an organized attack against Jews

   ⊂⊃ C a Jewish custom

   ⊂⊃ D a community in Russia

4. Based on paragraph 3, what were the feelings of some of the passengers on the ship?

   ⊂⊃ A regret and guilt

   ⊂⊃ B boredom and indifference

   ⊂⊃ C fear and rejoicing

   ⊂⊃ D anger and rage

Strategy 4 Use Information from the Text

Learn

Use information from the text to answer the question.

1. (Why) did Mary's (father) (go) to (Boston)? Use details from the text to support your answer.

   My Notes: Mary's father, ~~sent ship tickets~~,

   gone to Boston, Massachusetts, find work,

   ~~Mary boarded ship~~

   My Answer: Mary's father went to Boston to find

   work. He wanted to make enough money to buy

   tickets for his family to come to America.

- Look for and circle key words in the question.
- The word *why* tells you to look for the reasons for the actions of Mary's father.
- Read the text and **make notes** about why Mary's father went to Boston.

Reread the question and cross out any notes that do not apply to the question.

Answer the question in your own words.

Try It

Use information from the text to answer each question.

2. What was Mary's arrival in America like? Use details from the text to support your answer.

   My Notes: _____

   _____

   _____

   My Answer: _____

   _____

   _____

3. How did the letter to her uncle influence Mary's own life? Use details from the text to support your answer.

   My Notes: _____

   _____

   _____

   My Answer: _____

   _____

   _____

Strategy 5 Use Information from Graphics

Learn

Look at the graph on page 57. Use information from the graph to answer the question.

1. Based on the graph, (where) did (most) (immigrants) come from in the years (1901–1910)? Use details to support your answer.

> Look for and circle key words in the question.

To find the answer, I will *go back to the graph and look*

for where the most immigrants came from in 1901–1910.

My Answer: *About 8,000,000 immigrants came from*

Europe from 1901–1910. This was more immigrants than

from any other place.

> Look at page 57. Analyze the bar graph. Use details to support your answer.

Try It

Look at the graph on page 57. Use information from the graph to answer each question.

2. Based on the graph, where did the most immigrants come from in the years 1991–1998? Use details to support your answer.

To find the answer, I will _____

_____

My Answer: _____

_____

_____

3. Based on the graph, about how many immigrants came to the United States from Europe in the years 1991–1998? Use details to support your answer.

To find the answer, I will _____

_____

My Answer: _____

_____

_____

© Scott Foresman 5

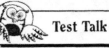
Strategy 6 Write Your Answer to Score High

Learn

Examine this sample done by an imaginary student named Dana. Analyze Dana's work.
Cross out unfocused information. What should she do to score higher?

1. (Why) did Mary's (father) (go) to (Boston)? Use details from
   the text to support your answer.

   | Dana circled key words in the question. |

   Dana's Notes: Mary's father, sent ship tickets,
   take family to United States, gone to Boston,
   Massachusetts, ~~Mary boarded ship~~

   | Dana's notes are incomplete. She needs to add more details. |

   Dana's Answer: Mary's father went to Boston.
   He wanted to send his family ship tickets so they
   could come to America. Finally Mary boarded the ship.

   | Dana's notes include unfocused information. |

   To score higher, Dana needs to _add that Mary's father went to America to find work to_
   make the answer complete, and cross out the unfocused information about Mary boarding
   the ship.

Try It

Examine this sample done by an imaginary student named Willy. Analyze Willy's work.
Cross out unfocused information. What should he do to score higher?

2. What was the trip to America like for Mary? Use details from the text to support
   your answer.

   Willy's Notes: slow-going, full of suffering, six weeks long, beheld Promise Land

   Willy's Answer: Mary's trip to America was full of suffering, and took a long time. Finally
   she saw the Promised Land.

   To score higher, Willy needs to _____

   _____

   _____

   _____

   _____

© Scott Foresman 5

The United States and the World

Directions: Read this biography. Then follow the directions on pages 65–70.

Dolores Huerta: 1930–

1   As a child, Dolores Huerta had watched her father try to earn a living as a migrant worker—moving from farm to farm, looking for enough work to feed his family. Migrant workers, many of whom were Mexican Americans, were usually paid very little, and often had no idea when or where they would find their next job.

2   In high school, Dolores was known as a girl who liked to talk a lot and always did well in class. In one class she received an A for every paper she wrote and every test she took. Yet she was very surprised when she saw her final grade, a C. The teacher did not believe that Dolores, a Mexican American, could do such good work on her own. Dolores later remembered this time in her life as a difficult one. She said: "I started noticing racism as a teenager and it took a long time to get over the feelings."

3   After college, Huerta became an elementary schoolteacher but soon decided that she wanted to work to improve the lives of migrant workers. "I couldn't stand seeing kids come to class hungry and needing shoes," she said.

4   Along with César Chávez, Huerta helped to create the first union for farm workers in the United States. The union, the National Farm Workers Association, successfully fought for such benefits as better pay, health insurance, and safer working conditions for farm workers. Today they also fight to reduce the exposure of farm workers to dangerous chemicals.

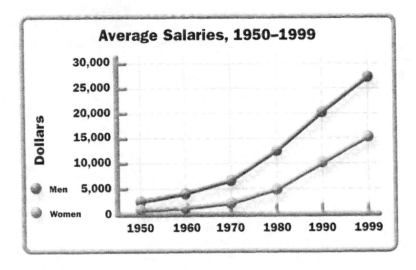

Average Salaries, 1950–1999

Strategy 1 Locate Key Words in the Question

Learn

Read the question. Circle the key words and complete the sentence.

1. (What) was the (life) of a (migrant) (farm) (worker) like?

   ⊂⊃ **A** A migrant farm worker moved from one country
   to another.

   ⊂⊃ **B** A migrant farm worker moved from farm to farm.

   ⊂⊃ **C** A migrant farm worker lived in Mexico.

   ⊂⊃ **D** A migrant farm worker always knew about the
   next job.

   I need to find out *what the life of a migrant farm*

   worker was like.

   > Circle key words.

   > Turn the question into a statement using key words.

Try It

Read each question. Circle the key words and complete each sentence.

2. Based on paragraph 2, why did Dolores receive a grade of C?

   ⊂⊃ **A** because her teacher did not believe she could do such good work

   ⊂⊃ **B** because she liked to talk a lot

   ⊂⊃ **C** because she received a C for all her papers and tests

   ⊂⊃ **D** because her teacher gave every student a C

   I need to find out _____

   _____

   _____

3. When did Huerta want to work to improve the lives of migrant workers?
   Use details from the text to support your answer.

   I need to find out _____

   _____

   _____

4. What did Huerta help create? Use details from the text to support your answer.

   I need to find out _____

   _____

   _____

Strategy 2 Locate Key Words in the Text

Learn

Read the question. Circle the key words and complete
the sentence.

- Look for and circle key words in the question.
- Look for and circle key words in the text that match key words in the question.

1. Based on paragraphs 1 and 4, how might (watching) her (father) work as a migrant farm worker have (influenced) (Dolores Huerta) to help (create) a (union) for farm workers? Use details from the text to support your answer.

   I found the answer in _paragraph 1, sentence 1; paragraph_

   4, sentences 1 and 2; and what I already know.

- The question asks you to tell how one experience causes another.
- You will have to **combine what you know with what the author tells you.**

Try It

Read each question. Circle the key words and complete each sentence.

2. Based on paragraph 3, when did Huerta decide to work to improve the lives of migrant workers?
   - ⬭ **A** soon after college
   - ⬭ **B** as far back as she could remember
   - ⬭ **C** when she was a teenager
   - ⬭ **D** after she helped create a union for farmers

   I found the answer in _____

   _____

3. Based on paragraph 3, why do you think Huerta left teaching? Use details from the text to support your answer.

   I found the answer in _____

   _____

4. Based on paragraph 4, what did Huerta help create? Use details from the text to support your answer.

   I found the answer in _____

   _____

Strategy 3 Choose the Right Answer

Learn

Cross out any choice you know is wrong. Next, go back to the text to rule out any other choices. Then mark your answer choice.

1. What was the life of a migrant farm worker like?

> ⬭ A ~~A migrant farm worker moved from one country to another.~~
>
> ⬤ B A migrant farm worker moved from farm to farm.
>
> ⬭ C ~~A migrant farm worker lived in Mexico.~~
>
> ⬭ D ~~A migrant farm worker always knew about the next job.~~

> You will have to **look in one place in the text**.

> Rule out the incorrect choices. Choose answer B because the text supports this choice.

Try It

Cross out any choice you know is wrong. Next, go back to the text to rule out any other choices. Then mark your answer choice.

2. Based on paragraph 2, why did Dolores receive a grade of C?

> ⬭ A because her teacher did not believe she could do such good work
>
> ⬭ B because she liked to talk a lot
>
> ⬭ C because she received a C for all her papers and tests
>
> ⬭ D because her teacher gave every student a C

3. When did Huerta decide to work to improve the lives of migrant workers?

> ⬭ A soon after college
>
> ⬭ B as far back as she could remember
>
> ⬭ C when she was a teenager
>
> ⬭ D after she helped create a union for farmers

4. What did Huerta help create?

> ⬭ A the first union for teachers in Mexico
>
> ⬭ B the first union for teachers in the United States
>
> ⬭ C the first union for farm workers in the United States
>
> ⬭ D the first union for farm workers in Mexico

© Scott Foresman 5

Strategy 4 **Use Information from the Text**

Learn

Use information from the text to answer the question.

1. (What) was the (life) of a (migrant) (farm) (worker) like? Use details from the text to support your answer.

   My Notes: ~~watched father~~, migrant worker, moving farm to farm, paid little, not know about next job

   My Answer: Life was hard for migrant farm workers. They moved from farm to farm. They did not get paid very much. They never knew if there would be work for them.

> - Look for and circle key words in the question.
> - The question is asking you to describe the life of a migrant farm worker.
> - Read the text and **make notes** about the life of a migrant farm worker.

> Reread the question and cross out any notes that do not apply to the question.

> Answer the question in your own words.

Try It

Use information from the text to answer the question.

2. Based on paragraph 2, why did Dolores receive a grade of C? Use details from the text to support your answer.

   My Notes: _____

   _____

   _____

   My Answer: _____

   _____

   _____

3. What could Huerta not stand when she was a teacher? Use details from the text to support your answer.

   My Notes: _____

   _____

   _____

   My Answer: _____

   _____

   _____

Strategy 5 Use Information from Graphics

Learn

Look at the line graph on page 64. Use information from the graph to answer the question.

1. Based on the graph, (what) was the (average) (salary) for (men) and for (women) in (1960)? Use details to support your answer.

   Look for and circle key words in the question.

   To find the answer, I will look at the points on the lines for 1960.

   My Answer: In 1960, the average salary for men was about 4,000 dollars. The average salary for women was about 1,000 dollars.

   Look at page 64. Analyze the line graph. Use details to answer the question.

Try It

Look at the line graph on page 64. Use information from the graph to answer each question.

2. Based on the graph, what was the average salary of men and women in 1999? Use details to support your answer.

   To find the answer, I will _____

   _____

   My Answer: _____

   _____

   _____

3. Based on the graph, in what year was the average salary for men and women almost the same? Use details to support your answer.

   To find the answer, I will _____

   _____

   My Answer: _____

   _____

   _____

© Scott Foresman 5

Strategy 6 Write Your Answer to Score High

Learn

Examine this sample done by an imaginary student named Jackie. Analyze Jackie's work. Cross out incorrect information. What should she do to score higher?

1. (Why) did (Huerta) (stop) (teaching)? Use details from the text to support your answer.

Jackie circled key words in the question.

   Jackie's Notes: schoolteacher, want to improve lives of workers, kids come to class hungry, need ~~shells~~

Jackie's information about workers is incomplete.

   Jackie's Answer: Huerta was a schoolteacher, but she wanted to improve worker's lives. Her students came to class hungry and needing shells. She did not want just to teach students. She wanted to improve lives.

Jackie's information about what the children need is incorrect.

   To score higher, Jackie needs to _make her details correct by replacing "shells" with "shoes,"_

   and add "migrant farm" to "workers" to make her answer complete.

Try It

Examine this sample done by an imaginary student named Anton. Analyze Anton's work. Cross out incorrect information. What should Anton do to score higher?

2. Based on paragraph 4, how did Huerta help farm workers? Use details from the text to support your answer.

   Anton's Notes: helped create first union for farm workers, fought against benefits, better pay, insurance, safer working conditions

   Anton's Answer: Huerta helped create the first union for farm workers. She fought against benefits, better pay, insurance, and safer working conditions.

   To score higher, Anton needs to _____

   _____

   _____

   _____

   _____

© Scott Foresman 5

Acknowledgements

Maps

Mapquest.com, an America Online, Inc. company

Illustrations

36 John Sandford
43 Robert Van Nutt

Photographs

Every effort has been made to secure permission and provide appropriate credit for photographic material. The publisher deeply regrets any omission and pledges to correct errors called to their attention in subsequent editions.

Unless otherwise acknowledged, all photographs are the property of Scott Foresman, a division of Pearson Education.

1 David Young-Wolff/PhotoEdit
15 Historical Society of Pennsylvania
22 © Dorling Kindersley
29 Rare Book and Special Collections/Library of Congress
29 North Wind Picture Archives